Buying Manorial Titles in England: a simple guide to the pitfalls

by

David Maximilian Cathmoir Nicoll
Baron of Bourn
Lord of the Manor of Adworthy

I hope you find this book useful.

© 2013, David Maximilian Cathmoir Nicoll

ISBN: 978-1-291-31303-1

The right of David Maximilian Cathmoir Nicoll to be identified as the author of this work has been asserted by him in accordance with the Copyright, Designs and Patents Act 1988, sections 77 and 78.

All rights reserved. No part of this book may be reproduced, stored in a retrieval system, or transmitted, in any form or by any means, electronic, mechanical, photocopying, recording or otherwise, without the consent of the copyright owners. Such a written permission must also be obtained before any part of this publication is stored in a retrieval system of any nature.

Disclaimer

While we have made efforts to provide accurate information, the law is always changing and affects each person differently. Statutes change and case law is continuously evolving. This information is no substitute for specific advice about you personally and we will not be liable to you if you rely on this information. Always seek qualified professional legal advice before engaging upon any activity related to a Lordship of the Manor title. This is a highly complex area of law and no single or general document will be able to accurately reflect the specific case of your situation.

This very short book, by its nature, can only serve as a basic introduction to an extremely complex area of law that is outside the scope of the knowledge of most general practitioners. If you are seeking advice in this area or are seeking to purchase a Lordship, 'caveat emptor' (Let the buyer beware).

TABLE OF CONTENTS

BACKGROUND..**1**

WHAT IS A MANOR?..**7**

WHAT IS A LORD OF THE MANOR?......................**15**

    1. The Manorial Property...*15*
    2. The Title of Lord...*17*
    3. The Lordship is Separate to the Land...............................*19*
    4. Succession to the Lordship..*21*

WHAT ISN'T A LORD OF THE MANOR?................**23**

    1. A Lord of the Manor is not a Peer of the Realm..........*23*
    2. A Lord of the Manor is not Necessarily One Person....*25*

PURCHASING A LORDSHIP TITLE..........................**27**

    1. The Small Matter of Using 'Filthy Lucre'....................*27*
    2. Why Would You Want a Lordship Title?....................*31*

THE LEGALITIES OF OWNING A MANORIAL LORDSHIP TITLE..**35**

    1. Adverse Possession...*37*
    2. Prescription (with Loss of Modern Grant)..................*41*
    3. Proprietary Estoppel..*45*
    4. Ownership of Deeds..*47*
        4.1   How far back must Deeds be held?..........*49*
        4.2   Presumption of Continuation.....................*51*
        4.3   What about the '15 year rule'...................*57*
    5. REGISTRATION OF TITLE WITH THE LAND REGISTRY..*61*
    6. Trademark Registration with the Intellectual
        Property office..*63*

MANORIAL INCIDENTS..65

1. SOME INTERESTING MANORIAL RIGHTS....................................*69*
    1.1 Foldage or Faldage.........................69
    1.2 Estovers, botes, furze and turbary..............70
    1.3 Pannage and mast........................70
    1.4 Merchet...................................70
    1.5 Assizes of Bread and Ale............................71
    1.6 Stocks, Pillory and Cucking Stool................72
    1.7 Gallows...73

SUMMARY..75

ABOUT THE AUTHOR..79

Background

The concept of "rights in land" as distinct from land itself was developed initially by the Roman Empire, and introduced to England with their arrival on our shores. However it was not until the Norman Conquest from 1066 that this became established as a standard part of English land law.

It was William the Conqueror who firmly established the key feudal maxim of *nulle terre sans seigneur* ("There is no land without its Lord"), which lasted for nearly a thousand years. The theory was that all land in England was held of the Crown, radical title having been acquired by conquest.

Prior to 1066, England had no centralized system of government. Power was in the hands of those rulers who owned the most land and controlled the most people. Chaos, disorganization, and power struggles ruled the land. After defeating Harold, William the Conqueror introduced feudalism as a system of government in England. This became a way of life and remained so for many centuries throughout England. Despite his victory, William still had to gain control of the English people before he could truly claim to be king. After all, he was an unpopular foreigner who fought his way into England and used force to maintain his control.

It was physically impossible for William to rule every part of the country himself. Not only was travel difficult and slow in the eleventh century, he was also still Duke of Normandy and he had to return to Normandy to maintain his control there and govern the country. Therefore, he had to leave the country for weeks at a time and needed a way of controlling England so that the people remained loyal. William divided England into very large plots of land – similar to our states today- and gave those to the men who fought for him in battle as a reward for their loyalty.

In exchange, these men swore an oath of loyalty to him, collected taxes in their area for him, and provided him with soldiers when needed. In the 11th century, an oath sworn on the Bible was very important. Few men would dare break the oath, as it would condemn them to Hell. Those who got these parcels of land were barons, earls, and dukes. In the terms of the feudal system, these men, the barons, were known as tenants-in-chief (although they held in fee) and they held directly from the Crown (*in capite*).

In return for their grants they were required to provide services. Typically the services would be the provision of knights to serve in the royal army ("knight service"); but they could also include other services, such as carrying the king's banner or holding his head when he felt seasick!

Even these pieces of land were large and difficult to govern. The barons further divided their land and gave smaller segments, the foundation of the English shires – or counties -- to trusted Norman knights who had also fought well in battle. Each knight received a segment of land to govern and swore an oath to the baron, collected taxes, and provided soldiers from his land when needed. These were called mesne tenants, and the process of sub-grants was called subinfeudation. Thus there was created what is called the feudal pyramid, with the king at the apex and the occupants of the land at the base.

Since the knights swore an oath to their baron, they in effect, swore an oath to the king as well. These subtenants worked to maintain law and order and could treat the people in their lands - or manors – harshly. They kept the people in their place and under control.

So, under the feudal system, tenants and subtenants rented their land in that they provided money or services to the real owner of all land-the king in turn they leased their parcels of land to the original populace.

That said, the changes introduced by William were not perhaps as far-reaching as some have claimed.

Manors were known in Anglo-Saxon times. Within the manor the lord kept land for his own use, known as demesne land. He would also grant out land to tenants, in return for services. Typically these were agricultural services; and the tenants held by customary tenure. William solidified some of the arrangements, and it is certainly true that, in the course of William's reign, all the greatest estates and all the highest Offices in England were transferred from English to Norman owners. However the transfer of land was certainly not so great as has often been fancied. The notion that every Englishman was turned out of hearth and home is a mere dream. The actual occupants of the soil remained very generally undisturbed.

So, for example, Lady Godiva - the Anglo Saxon wife of Earl Leofric of Mercia - was a significant landowner both before and after the Norman Conquest of England. Indeed, she also holds the distinction of being only major woman named in the Domesday survey as being a landowner in her own right.

That is not, of course, to deny the obvious shift in the powerbase of the country at large. However the great confiscation of lands which is such a marked characteristic of William's reign overall was undoubtedly gradual, an evolution rather than a revolution.

This evolution is a mark of English law in general, and feudal tenure in particular. For example the concept of feudal tenure itself over time evolved into the form of tenure known as copyhold, and this, in turn, was eventually abolished as late as 1922. With the exception of copyhold and frankalmoign (the landholdings of the Church), all other tenures were converted into free & common socage (i.e. for the payment of rent) by the Tenures Abolition Act of 1660, and frankalmoign was also abolished in 1922.

THIS PAGE IS INTENTIONALLY BLANK

What is a Manor?

As Christopher Jessel succinctly puts it in his book *The Law of the Manor* (2012)[1];

> "There is no formal legal definition of a manor". They varied in size, composition and value from the very beginning, and a 'typical' manor never existed. In that sense, every manor is a unique thing. However there were some things that marked them out.

In mediaeval times the manor was the nucleus of English rural life. It was an administrative unit of an extensive area of land. The whole of it was owned originally by the lord of the manor. He lived in the big house called the manor house. Attached to it were many acres of grassland and woodlands called the park. These were the "demesne lands" which were for the personal use of the lord of the manor. Dotted all round were the enclosed homes and land occupied by the "tenants of the manor." They held them by copyhold tenure. Their titles were entered in the court rolls of the manor. They were nearly

---

[1] Jessel, C. (2012) The Law of the Manor 2nd Edition, London: Wildy, Simmonds and Hill Publishing

equivalent to freehold, but the tenants were described as "tenants of the manor."

The rest of the manorial lands were the "waste lands of the manor." The tenants of the manor had the right to graze their animals on the waste lands of the manor. This was held by the lord of the manor, although it might be held subject to customary rights, such as rights of common.

This perhaps lies at the heart of what a 'manor' was - partly about land, partly about social status, partly about control.

Although the demesne land was personal to the lord of the manor, nevertheless he sometimes granted to the tenants of the manor the right to graze their animals on it, or they acquired it by custom. In such a case their right to graze on the demesne land was indistinguishable from their right to graze on the waste lands of the manor, so long as it remained open to them and uncultivated, although there might be hedges and gates to keep the cattle from straying. So much so that their rights over it became known as a "right of common" and the land became known as "common land."

In the course of time, however, the lordship of the manor often became severed from the lands of the manor. This was where the lord of the manor sold off parcels of the land to purchasers. He might, for instance, sell off the demesne lands and convey them as a distinct property. Thenceforward the land ceased to form part of the manor and was held by a freeholder[2]. But no such conveyance could adversely affect the rights of common of those who were entitled to them as tenants of the manor or otherwise. No lord of the manor could, by alienation, deprive those entitled of their rights over it or in respect of it[3]. In conjunction with the separate nature of the land of the manor and the title and the rights of the manor, it is also worth noting that land acquired outside a manor cannot be annexed to a manor, even if the tenants agree to the annexation[4].

One of the essential ingredients of a manor was its court. The principal court was the court baron, which amongst other things settled property disputes between the tenants of the manor. It also dealt with

---

[2] see Delacherois v Delacherois (1864) 11 HL Cas 62, 102-103 by Lord St Leonards

[3] see Swayne's case (1609) 8 Co Rep 63a and R v Duchess of Buccleuch (1704) 1 Salk 358. (quoted by Denning J in Corpus Christi College Oxford v Gloucestershire County Council [1983] QB 360)

[4] The Compleat Copyholder by Sir Edward Coke, 1650, Section 31

succession to copyhold land by recording changes of copyholder. The free tenants of the manor were the jury. The suitors were also drawn from among the free tenants. Since no one can be both suitor and juror, it followed that the court could not be held once the number of free tenants fell below two.

As Blackstone put it[5]:

> "This court is an inseparable ingredient of every manor; and if the number of suitors should so fail, as not to leave sufficient to make a jury or homage, that is two tenants at the least, the manor itself is lost." In the modern law a manor that has been lost in this fashion is known as a reputed manor. As Justice Levison[6] stated, "most manors today are reputed manors. The Lordship rights attaching to a reputed manor are similar to those attaching to a true manor."

At a very early time in medieval England the Lord of the Manor exercised or claimed certain jurisdictional rights over his tenants and bondsmen concerning the administration of his manor and exercised those rights through his court baron. However this court

---

[5] 2 Bl Comm 91

[6] Crown Estate Commissioners v Roberts [2008] 2 EGLR 165

had no power to deal with criminal acts. They dealt purely with civil matters relating to the Manor: tenancies, succession, and so on.

Criminal jurisdiction could, however, be granted to a trusted lord by the Crown by means of an additional franchise to give him the prerogative rights he owed feudally to the king. The most important of these was the "view of frankpledge", by which tenants were held responsible for the actions of others within a grouping of ten households. The most serious crimes were committed to the King's Justices. In some cases, the local Lord was also granted the "right of gallows" - the ability to impose capital punishment for crimes. In the later Middle Ages the Lord, when exercising these powers, gained the name of leet which was a jurisdiction of a part of a county, hence the franchise was of court leet.

Edward I established a sharp distinction between the court baron, exercising strictly manorial rights, and the court leet, depending for its jurisdiction upon royal franchise. However in many areas it became customary for the two courts to meet together.

It also developed as a means of proactively ensuring that standards in such matters as sales of food and drink, and agriculture, were adhered to.

As an example, the Alcester Court Leet contained the following wording:

> "To enquire regularly and periodically into the proper condition of watercourses, roads, paths, and ditches; to guard against all manner of encroachments upon the public rights, whether by unlawful enclosure or otherwise; to preserve landmarks, to keep watch and ward in the town, and overlook the common lands, adjust the rights over them, and restraining in any case their excessive exercise, as in the pasturage of cattle; to guard against the adulteration of food, to inspect weights and measures, to look in general to the morals of the people, and to find a remedy for each social ill and inconvenience. To take cognisance of grosser crimes of assault, arson, burglary, larceny, manslaughter, murder, treason, and every felony at common law".

The court generally sat only a few times each year, sometimes just annually. A matter was introduced into the court by means of a "presentment", from a local man or from the jury itself. Penalties were in the form of fines or imprisonment. Attendance at the Court Leet was often compulsory for those under its jurisdiction and some Courts still levy a nominal fine for non-attendance, 2p for example in the case of Laxton.

The court leet began to decline in the fourteenth century, being superseded by the more modern county Justices of the Peace and ultimately magistrates' courts, but in many cases courts leet operated until nearly the middle of the nineteenth century as a form of civil administration with a similar role to borough freemen or parish vestrymen.

However Courts Leet survived for formal purposes well into modern times, until their legal criminal jurisdiction was abolished by section 23 of the Administration of Justice Act 1977. One exception was allowed, namely the Court Leet for the manor of Laxton, Nottinghamshire, which was allowed to keep its jurisdiction to administer and settle disputes over the open field system of farming which still operates in that area.

THIS PAGE IS INTENTIONALLY BLANK

What is a Lord of the Manor?

The importance of all this for purchasers of a Manorial Title is this - a manorial title was part of the rights *package* (a seigniory) that went with a Manor, separate to the physical land that composed the manor, or the manor house. Thus the right to the title is classed as an *incorporeal hereditament*. In simple terms: incorporeal - not "physical", hereditament - can be inherited. The land itself, by contract, is a *physical hereditament*.

1. The Manorial Property

In England, the Lord of a Manor is a recognised as someone who owns a form of property, the manor, which is made up of two elements that may exist separately or be combined and may be held in parts (known as moieties):

- the manorial, consisting of the manor and its land; and
- the seignory, rights granted to the holder of the manor which includes the rights to the title "Lord of the Manor", with origins in the Roman concept of dignitas.

THIS PAGE IS INTENTIONALLY BLANK

2. The Title of Lord

A title similar to such a lordship is known in French as Seigneur du Manoir, Gutsherr in German, godsherre in Norwegian and Swedish, ambachtsheer in Dutch and signore or vassallo in Italian. In Italy, particularly in the Norman Kingdom of Sicily, the feudal title signore was used.

Historically a lord of the manor might be a tenant-in-chief if he held a capital manor directly from the Crown; otherwise he was a "mesne lord" if he did not hold directly from the Crown, yet had his own tenants.

Holding the right to a manor was a critical part of the feudal system – partly because the tenure denoted great honour, but mainly because the Lord carried heavy responsibilities, including providing knights and soldiers for the king's army.

The owner of a lordship of the manor can be described as [Personal Name], Lord/Lady of the Manor of [Placename], sometimes shortened to Lord or Lady of [Placename] or even Lord or Lady [Placename].

THIS PAGE IS INTENTIONALLY BLANK

3. The Lordship is separate to the land

There is still, however, a very big confusion in many people's minds about the title Lord of the Manor.

This is because the title (as we have seen so far) arose out of the person's ownership of a manor – a piece of physical land. As such, over time, the two items have been 'conflated' in many people's minds. They are considered to be the same thing.

This is not the case!

The seignory (that is the rights), whilst often spoken about as being *'attached'* to the land' are in fact separate. They are only '*linked'* to the land.

This separation is important, and we will discuss the importance of this later when we come to talk about the need for the Title Deeds to be correctly written up. But the heart of the matter is this:

Throughout the whole of English history, except for the period 1881 to 1925, when speaking about the manor you were ONLY speaking about the physical land. The Lordship had to be specifically referred to if that was meant. Indeed, if a document does not refer to the seigneury but only to the manor, then the law holds that the seignory is specifically EXCLUDED from that document[7].

This is why I started the book with a discussion about 'rights in land' as differentiated from 'rights over land'. They are separate assets, separate ideas, and separate items of property. Throughout history they were always treated as separate pieces of history. It is only in the relatively modern period (1881-1925) that this was brought together, and although they have been separated again many people still wrongly assume they refer to the same thing.

---

[7] Rooke v Lord Kensington (1856) 2 K&J 753, 772

4. Succession to the Lordship

Succession to the Lordship was originally a complicated process that involved significantly more than 'mere' inheritance. When an English tenant-in-chief died, his or her land temporarily escheated (i.e. reverted) to the demesne of the crown until the heir paid a sum of money (a relief), and was then able to take possession (livery of seisin) of the lands.

However, if the heir was under age (under 21 for a male heir, under 14 for an heiress) they would be subject to a feudal wardship where the custody of their lands and the right to arrange their marriage passed to the monarch, until they came of age. The wardship and marriage was not usually kept in Crown hands, but was sold, often simply to the highest bidder, unless outbid by the next of kin.

When an heir came of age, he or she passed out of wardship but could not enter upon their inheritance until, like all heirs of full age on inheritance, they had sued out their livery. In either case, the process was complicated.

Eventually a warrant was issued for the livery to pass under the Great Seal. This was such a revenue generator for the Crown that between 1540 and 1646, a special office, The Court of Wards and

Liveries administered the funds received from the wardships, marriages and the granting of livery.

Since the Abolition of Tenures Act 1660, succession to the Lordship is simply a matter of conveyance of the title using similar rules to land law. No 'fines' or 'fees' have to be paid other than the purchase price and legal costs for the transfer deeds.

What isn't a Lord of the Manor?

1. A Lord of the Manor is not a Peer of the Realm

The 'problem' of what the Lord of the Manor is - and is not - has confused some of the brightest people for several centuries. As Sir William Betham, Ulster King of Arms, said nearly two hundred years ago[8]:

> "The difficulty of rightly understanding the real character of English titles of dignity has thus, in a great measure, arisen from confounding persons possessed of feudal seignories in ancient times, whether called earldoms, honours, or baronies, with peers, or lords of parliament, which although distinct, and altogether different in their nature and origin, yet time and disuse having gradually obliterated all precise recollection of their functions, peers, or lords of parliament, have been confounded with the ancient earls and barons, merely because they bore the same names …. by confounding the personal dignity of a peer in parliament, inherent in the blood of the possessor, with a title or name attached to

---

[8] Betham, Sir W. J. (1830), Dignities, Feudal and Parliamentary, & the constitutional legislature of the United Kingdom, Volume 1, London: Thomas & William Boone

> land, merely judicial, having little, if any legislative character"

The feudal Lord, Baron and Earl - whilst quite rightly called "Lord", "Baron" and "Earl" - are quite clearly NOT the same (at least now) as the Lords, Barons and Earls meeting in parliament and created by Letters Patent.

This is why some people, quoting the Honours (Prevention of Abuses) Act 1925, wrongly state that you "cannot buy a Lordship".

That Act prevents the purchase of Peerages of the United Kingdom. It was brought in after the Liberal Party government of David Lloyd George, (later 1st Earl Lloyd-George of Dwyfor) was embroiled in a widespread and long-term sale of honours, for the personal financial gain of the Prime Minister. It is also the Act under which the "Cash for Honours" row of the early twenty-first century was investigated - showing that the honour and integrity of politicians doesn't seem to have changed much over the last hundred years.

What the Act explicitly does NOT do is affect the purchase and sale of feudal titles, which are very different titles completely.

2. A Lord of the Manor is not necessarily only one person

Another key difference between a feudal Lord, Baron or Earl and one of the "Lords in Parliament" is that whilst there can only ever be one Peer of a particular title at any one time, there could be a number of different holders of the same feudal title.

How can this be? After all there can only ever be one owner of a piece of land. So how can several people be the Lord over that land?

The answer lies in the delights of inheritance law. A "manor" or a "barony" or even an "earldom" in the feudal context was made up of a parcel of land of varying sizes. Usually, the eldest son inherited all the property, and in those cases life was simple. But in many cases, a feudal Lord died only having daughters, and each of these may have inherited a part of the manor. So for example, Agatha de Radendon inherited one-thirty-sixth of the Barony of Bourn in the late thirteenth century. This was later made up to an eighteenth when she married her husband who had also inherited one-thirty-sixth of the Barony. However, despite inheriting only a fraction of the feudal lands, she was still fully entitled to be called the Baron of Bourn.

As I J Sanders explains[9]:

> "fractions of a baronia which was divided between co-heirs maintained their identity. Thus it was possible for a tenant-in-chief to be the lord of fractions of several different baronies if his ancestors had married coheiresses. The tenure of even the smallest fraction conferred baronial status on the lord of those lands."

These fractions are called moieties. For them to be valid in so far as 'Lord of the Manor' titles are concerned, they must have been created prior to 1290. After then, splitting up a manor's land did not split up the Lordship Title which remained 'inviolate'. It remained in as many 'pieces' as existed at 1289 – or fewer if heirs brought their shares back together, because once reunited they couldn't then be re-split.

---

[9] Sanders, I.J. (1960), English Baronies: A study of their origin and descent 1086-1327, Oxford: The Clarendon press

Purchasing a Lordship Title

1. The small matter of using 'filthy lucre'

Some people have an odd attitude with regards to the purchasing a Lord of the Manor title. This reflects on both the practice of purchasing a title, and on the fact that it is a Manor.

However, as you saw earlier, to obtain a Lordship of the Manor in history you had to purchase it on the death of the previous owner, even if you were the legal heir.

Indeed, the use of money was simply a peaceful alternative to the original method of taking control of the Lordship, which was by force of arms. As so well put in the film *A Knight's Tale*[10]:

> "How did the nobles become noble? They took it .... at the point of a sword".

In terms of land based assets this is understandable, but for much of history it was also an acceptable method of gaining a Peerage. Current Baronets of England, for example, obtained their titles originally

---

[10] http://www.subzin.com/quotes/A+Knight's+Tale/
How+did+the+nobles+become+noble+in+the+first+place

by purchase from King James I for the sum of £1,095. A Baronetcy of Scotland and Nova Scotia cost 2,000 marks.

Furthermore, the purchase of Peerages was (until the start of the 20th century) perfectly normal. The Honours (Prevention of Abuses) Act 1925 was introduced not because the general principle was wrong, but because it was being abused excessively.

This was because the Liberal Party government of David Lloyd George (later 1st Earl Lloyd-George of Dwyfor) was embroiled in a widespread and long-term sale of honours, for the personal financial gain of the Prime Minister, in a then-legal abuse of the Prime Minister's powers of patronage.

Of course, this didn't stop the behavior. It simply drove it "under the radar". As recently as March 2006, the Metropolitan Police confirmed that they were investigating possible breaches of the Act (the so-called 'cash for honours' scandal). A total of £14 million in "loans" were given by wealthy individuals to Labour during the 2005 general election campaign and four of these men were subsequently nominated for Peerages.

In many ways, the purchase of Lord of the Manor titles (as they come without a seat in the legislature and nowadays have a mainly historic, cultural and community focus) have considerably more status and honour than a Peerage.

In many cases they also come with significantly more heritage – especially since no new manors could have been created since 1289, whereas the latest hereditary peerage was created as recently as 29 April 2011 (when Prince William became the Duke of Cambridge) and the last 'commoner' appointed to a peerage was on 24 February 1984 (former Prime Minister Harold Macmillan, appointed first Earl of Stockton).

THIS PAGE IS INTENTIONALLY BLANK

2. Why would you want a Lordship title?

People acquire Lordships of the Manor for many reasons.

- For some it is about family history - restoring a manor to a family line where it was once held in antiquity
- For some it is about a sense of belonging - creating a tangible attachment to a place that is dear to their hearts
- For some it is about opening doors for their charitable activities
- For some it is about simply owning something that brings a smile to their face every time they open their passport or look at their driving license

As Christopher Jessel points out,

> "The meaning of manor and its place in society has changed over the centuries … Its main feature was originally social, administrative and economic. Later it became a piece of property producing an income and other benefits such as sporting privileges. **Now it has become a luxury item**." *(my emphasis)*

As to their value, titles are sold for a wide range of prices. HM Revenue and Customs states[11]:

> "Although many of the pecuniary rights of the Lords of the Manor were abolished by the Law of Property Act 1922, a variety of privileges remain with them, including rights associated with minerals, the ownership of documents of title, and - perhaps the greatest attraction - the right to call oneself Lord of the Manor. Manorial lordships are saleable, and their average values can be in excess of £10,000."

For example, Chris Eubank paid £45,000 back in 1996 for the title Lord of the Manor of Brighton. French international footballer Djibril Cisse became Lord of the Manor of Frodsham when he bought a manor house in Cheshire that came with the title. The property is rumoured to have cost a cool £2 million.

---

[11] IHTM23194 - Special valuation matters: Lordships of the Manor and Baronial Titles.
http://www.hmrc.gov.uk/manuals/ihtmanual/IHTM23194.htm

People often buy titles to bring the title back to the land and link it in with a house they have bought. Some buy them because they have a great affinity with a particular place. Others have found the title a useful gateway for their charitable foundations and activities.

Many of the feudal Lords I personally know make use of their titles in helping community organisations and charities raise funds and make a difference to people's lives. This ranges from leading fundraising appeals for local hospices, to helping isolated and vulnerable individuals in their homes. Sometimes this is done in a 'serious' manner and sometimes they make use of the 'fun' side of it at local fairs and markets to help create community interaction.

At the end of the day none of these change them as a person. None of these make the owner a better being. But they are powerful gateways to conversations. They make things happen. And in fact many people find that as they take ownership of their Lordship Title, they do begin to change as people – taking more notice of their responsibilities as well as their 'rights'.

THIS PAGE IS INTENTIONALLY BLANK

The Legalities of Owning a Manorial Lordship Title

To own a title, the right to use the title has to be ***legally passed*** from one individual to another. This is important not only to allow the peaceable enjoyment of the title, but also because the Lord of the Manor also owns the manorial waste of the manor.

Of course, for it to be legally passed to you, the person claiming the title in the first place must themselves actually own the asset – otherwise they are committing fraud – taking money off of you for what effectively amounts to a 'bag of beans'.

Unfortunately legal ownership is more complicated than you might think.

There are many people who CLAIM they own a 'Lordship of the Manor' and want to sell it to you.

The reality is that all except one seller (as at the time of writing) use one or more of the following methods to claim they own the title to a Lordship of the Manor.

Each of these 'claims to title' have been proven to be simply FICTIONAL. They don't exist. They have no legal validity.

THIS PAGE IS INTENTIONALLY BLANK

1. *Adverse Possession*

Some have argued that title can be claimed by the use of adverse possession.

Adverse Possession is a process by which premises can change ownership. It is a governed by The Law of Property Act 1925 concerning the title to real property (land and the fixed structures built upon it). By adverse possession, title to another's real property can be acquired without compensation, by holding the property in a manner that conflicts with the true owner's rights for a specified period.

However, a manor or lordship is outside the definition of "land" in section 132 of the Land Registration Act 2002. Manors were deliberately removed from the definition[12].

This definition is different to that to be found in section 205(ix) of the Law of Property Act 1925 which expressly included a manor or lordship, or to that to be found in section 3(viii) of the Land Registration Act 1925 which also expressly included a manor.

---

[12] see paragraph 3.20 of Law Commission Report No 254

Additionally, s.131(1) of the Land Registration Act 2002 provides that, for the purposes of the Act, land is in the possession of the proprietor of a registered estate in land if it is physically in his possession. Lordship of the Manor titles have no physical existence, so it is difficult to find circumstances in which someone could claim to be in physical possession of it. Indeed, some have gone so far as to state that there is NO AUTHORITY to suggest that an incorporeal hereditament can be adversely possessed in the way a physical thing can be possessed.

In addition, adverse possession only works if there is a means to extinguish any potential claim by another person, and this is established through statutes of limitation.

The first statute of limitation was the Statute of Merton in 1235 which limited actions for the recovery of land by writ to 70 years. Further statutes including Henry VIIIs 1540 statute was repealed by the Statute Law Repeals Act 1887 and the Limitation Act of 1623 was repealed by the Statute Law Repeals Act 1986. In addition the Crown Suits Act 1769 as amended by the Crown Suits Act 1862 was repealed by the Limitation Act 1939.

These days the only statute to cover limitation of actions for land is the Limitation Act 1980 which only covers REAL land. Section 38(1) of this Act is clear that it does not apply to incorporeal hereditaments. This is also true of the 1939 act.

Further, the decision of the High Court in Cocker v Fothergill [1819] 2 B & Ald 652 is authority for the proposition that an incorporeal hereditament is incapable of possession.

Further, as pointed out by the Adjudicator in Land Registry case 2007/1124[13] "there is no merit in these submissions. Incorporeal hereditaments are not capable of being adversely possessed.

As Stephen Jourdan QC's Adverse Possession puts it:

> "Claims to incorporeal hereditaments ... are governed by the law of prescription ... which operate[s] on different principles to the law of adverse possession."

As a result of this clear statement, Adverse Posession is NOT a method available for the transfer of a Lordship of the Manor title.

---

[13] Burton & Banford v Walker & others (2010) Land Registry Ref 2007/1124

THIS PAGE IS INTENTIONALLY BLANK

2. Prescription (with Loss of Modern Grant)

Commonly prayed in aid by those who are seeking to establish an easement by prescription, the doctrine of lost modern grant usefully avoids difficulties that exist in establishing prescription at common law or under the *Prescription Act 1832*. It has also been used as an attempt to claim Lordship of the Manor titles on the basis that in English Law there is a strong policy bias in favour of the legitimacy of a user which has been exercised de facto over extended periods of time.

Developed in the eighteenth century and confirmed by the House of Lords in the nineteenth[14], it survived an attack on the ground that it was incompatible with the provisions of the European Convention on Human Rights[15] and is used by claimants asserting a legal right to carry on an activity enjoyed without interruption for years past, but unable to show a documentary title. The user must exercise their use nec vi, nec clam and nec precario - without force, without secrecy and without permission.

---

[14] Dalton v Angus & Co.(1881) 6 App. Cas. 740

[15] Mills v M.I. Developments Ltd.[2002] E.W.C.A. Civ. 1576

As its name suggests, where a claimant can rely successfully on the doctrine to establish the right claimed, it is because a grant to him or his predecessor of that right is presumed to have been made, but is now lost.

With reference to the use of prescription, the adjudication in Burton & Banford v Walker & others[16] was forceful. Not only was it not possible, but the Adjudicator stated,

> "This is a fictional lawful grant".

This is not because the doctrine does not exist, but because in the context of Manorial titles, it has simply not been possible for a new grant of a lordship lawfully to be made since the Statute of Quia Emptores 1290 brought to an end sub-infeudation. Originally, Quia Emptores allowed the Crown to create new manors. However by 1585 this had also been removed[17]:

> "A manor cannot be created at this day, neither by a common person nor by the Queen."

---

[16] Burton & Banford v Walker & others (2010) Land Registry Ref 2007/1124

[17] Morris v Smith and Paget (1585) Cro. Eliz. 38 stated

As Prescription operates to create a new title, Quia Emptores says this cannot be done.

As a result of this clear statement, Prescription is NOT a method available for the transfer of a Lordship of the Manor title.

THIS PAGE IS INTENTIONALLY BLANK

3. Proprietary Estoppel

Proprietary Estoppel has also been tried as a way of claiming a Lordship of the Manor title. A proprietary estoppel may arise if:

a. one party represents that he or she is transferring an interest in land to another, but what is done has no legal effect, **or**
b. merely promises at some time in the future to transfer land or an interest in land to another, **and**
c. knows that the other party will spend money or otherwise act to his or her detriment in reliance on the supposed or promised transfer

In <u>Willmott v Barber (1880) 15 Ch D 96</u>, Fry J considered that five elements had to be established before proprietary estoppel could operate:

1. the claimant must have made a mistake as to his legal rights;
2. the claimant must have done some act of reliance;
3. the defendant, the possessor of a legal right, must know of the existence of his own right which is inconsistent with the right claimed by the claimant;

4. the defendant must know of the claimant's mistaken belief; and
5. the defendant must have encouraged the claimant in his act of reliance.

Although proprietary estoppel was only traditionally available in disputes affecting title to real property, it has now gained limited acceptance in other areas of law.

Of course for this to operate, point 3 points out that the legal right must exist in the first place. Therefore Proprietory Estoppel does not prove the right exists, but merely operates in the context of a transfer of ownership.

Proprietary Estoppel therefore does not establish the existence of the legal right to the Lordship of the Manor title.

4. Ownership of Deeds

Ownership of a title must therefore be proved by a set of deeds.

For this method , a basic principle of conveyancing is relied upon: If a Manorial title is to be passed on a conveyance, it has to be **expressly conveyed**.

General words are not enough. It cannot be conveyed by implication from other language in the conveyance[18].

In other words, the deeds available on transfer of the Lordship of the Manor must refer specifically to the Lordship of the Manor title.

It might be argued, on the authority of Lord Hardwicke[19] that general words would be sufficient to pass title to a manor, but that case was only authority for the proposition that general words would suffice when land was being settled, rather than conveyed in the modem sense.

This requirement ceased to apply to transactions after the coming into force of the Conveyancing Act 1881.

---

[18] Rooke v Lord Kensington (1856) 2 K&J 753, 772

[19] Norris v Le Neve (1744) 3 Atk 82

Section 62(3) of the Law of Property Act 1925 later provided that:

> "A conveyance of a manor shall be deemed to include and shall by virtue of this Act operate to convey, with the manor all ... hereditaments whatsoever, to the manor appertaining or reputed to appertain, or, at the time of conveyance, demised, occupied, or enjoyed with the same, or reputed or known as part, parcel, or member thereof."

However it should be noted that the sale of a manor house of itself does not convey the sale of a manor or the title, a point specifically referenced in Burton & Banford v Walker & others.

So any Deeds held must, as a matter of principle, refer to the manor and to the title and rights of the lord of the manor SEPARATELY, and must EXPLICITLY state they are being transferred, EXCEPT during the period from 1881 to 1925.

That window of 44 years were the ONLY ones during which the title and rights of a manor could be transferred along with the manor itself without being explicitly referred to.

4.1 How far back must Deeds be held?

The primary requirement is that all the deeds, correctly written must be available until the commencement of the Manor – which in many cases dates back to before the Norman Conquest of England in 1066.

Very soon in English history it was recognised that this proof was very burdensome. So in English law and its derivatives, the concept of owning a manor since time immemorial - "a time before legal history and beyond legal memory" - was established. If you could prove ownership since time immemorial, you didn't have to go all the way back to the formation of the Manor.

The Statute of Westminster set the baseline date for "time immemorial" as 3 September 1189, the date of the coronation of King Richard I.

Some differences now exist in branches of the law, and for heraldry it is set at the Norman invasion, but for the purposes of Lordship of the Manor titles, if they were created prior to 6 July 1189 proof only needs to go back to that date and not before.

THIS PAGE IS INTENTIONALLY BLANK

4.2 Presumption of continuation

English Law recognises that the practicalities of this render it virtually impossible for anyone to hold correctly written deeds going back nearly 1000 years.

In particular, reference should be made to the decision of Lawrence J, as he then was[20], providing authority for the proposition that prior to the enactment of the amendment to the Law of Property Act 1922, there was no obligation on the lord of a manor to retain the manorial records in his possession. It was to reverse that decision that the amending legislation was introduced.

It therefore follows that any records could have been destroyed, or parted with, long before 1924. In other words it is highly unlikely that anyone holds manorial records dating back to 1189. Therefore the presumption of continuation is sometimes used to 'bridge the gaps'.

In the Land Registry case of Burton & Banford v Walker & others the Deeds were correctly held back to 1836, and the presumption of continuation was relied upon to claim correct ownership of the

---

[20] in Beaumont v Jeffery [1925] Ch 1

Lordship of the Manor title back to the last available recorded dates.

In addition, as a result of <u>Baxter v Mannion [2010] EWHC 573 (Ch)</u>, any challenge to the title had to prove that title was invalid. As such rather than having to prove the Title was held, challengers had to prove the legal case why it was NOT held. This set an important precedent for Lordship of the Manor titles, as it resulted in a very clear statement of much of the law that applies to the legal transfer of title.

It was clear from the paperwork in the Burton & Banford case that whilst the Lordship of the Manor had been actively claimed in some form up until 1598, there was no reference to the Lordship from that year until it was claimed again in the nineteenth century. There were therefore arguments presented over whether this was relevant.

It was noted that the various assets of the manor were broken up and sold off in the period after 1605. As a result even if the Lordship existed after 1605, it was no more than a reputed lordship. This is because there were no longer two free tenants holding of it who could sit in a court baron. The conveyancing requirements for transferring a reputed lordship were therefore not met. There was no documentary evidence that the lordship was conveyed thereafter.

It was noted that here is no document showing that the property bought by Burton & Banford was the manor house to which the lordship is appurtenant. It was also noted that the Victoria Counties History specifically refers to the sale of the manor in 1598 and observes that no manor appears to have been claimed since that time. It was also noted that an indenture dated 1 October 1804 makes reference to the lordship of Ireby, and that this appeared to be the first written reference since 1598.

It was noted that from 1806 there are a series of written appointments of gamekeepers by people claiming the right as lords of the manors. However there is no record of gamekeepers being appointed in this manor before 1806, yet lords of the manor were given power to appoint gamekeepers by section 4 of the Game Act 1706. Nor was the appointment of gamekeepers the exclusive preserve of lords of the manor[21].

In addition, whilst the Lordship of the Manor title itself had been claimed, the rights associated with that Lordship between 1836 and 2004 had not been exercised by the Lord of the Manor – and had in fact been exercised by either by the village meeting, the

---

[21] see section 5 of the Game Act 1831

parish council, or an informal committee of the grazers over that period.

With all this history, the claimants to the title of the Lordship of the Manor asked the courts to take into account both the presumption of continuity[22] and that it is not necessary in order to prove the existence of a manor to produce the court rolls or any documentary proof of the holding of courts and that reputation alone is admissible[23]. There was also a reliance on the reputation of the authors of various items of documentary evidence, which is admissible under section 7(3)(b)(i) of the Civil Evidence Act 1995. The basis was that this would override the lack of evidence since 1605.

The judgement was that if, ever since the 1836 stinting agreement, the powers and functions of the Lord of the Manor had been regularly exercised and continuously regulated for the benefit of those with rights of common and the local community, and that such continuity had been acceded to by the local community, the court would have been prepared to allow the claim (despite the gaps of evidence) as it amounted to exceptional circumstances. But that

---

[22] Phipson on Evidence 16th edition paragraphs 7-20 and following

[23] 12(1) Halsbury's Laws 4th edition re-issue 698

had not been the case. Until Mr Burton and Ms Bamford claimed the title no one appears to have acted as Lord of the Manor for over a century. As a result the claim to the title of the Lordship of the Manor was closed and the title was deemed to have ceased to exist somewhere between 1598 and 1605.

In the absence of continuous, correctly written deeds of transfer, therefore, a Court Order is required to prove current title through reliance on the presumption of history. However even with such a Court Order the title remains challengeable on many fronts and may in fact be closed by the courts.

THIS PAGE IS INTENTIONALLY BLANK

4.3 What about the '15 year rule'?

There are some solicitors, and even some 'experts' in the field, who claim that 15 years of title deeds are enough.

This is actually not a 'rule'. As Christopher Jessel points out[24];

> "the object of an unregistered title is to produce a chain of deeds and events which give a complete picture of successive owners as far back as is necessary to show that the chain is better than any other. Each successive owner's title therefore depends on that of his predecessor. In practice, conveyancers will accept relatively short title. Under the Law of Property Act 1969, s 23, amending the Law of Property Act 1925, s44 (1), a title beginning with a good root not less than 15 years old is normally acceptable. A good root is one on which a solicitor would have been expected to investigate the title for a similar earlier period (before 1969 it was 30 years and before 1926 it was 40 years), namely a

---

[24] Jessel, C. (2012) The Law of the Manor 2nd Edition, London: Wildy, Simmonds and Hill Publishing

dealing for money that is a sale or mortgage."

Unfortunately this approach contains a number of major flaws when it comes to claiming a Lord of the Manor title.

Firstly it relies on a *chain of ownership* - and one or two people do not make a chain.

Secondly, it relies on *the original holder having good title* - which is of itself easily challengeable in the case of an unregistered title.

Thirdly, it relies on their having been a *dealing for money* in the chain - which in most cases we have seen relating to transactions relying on this "rule" does not exist. A statutory declaration, which is often used in this context, does not provide evidence of a 'deal for money'.

Fourthly, following the Land Registration Act 2002, whilst a Lordship of the Manor is technically land for conveyancing purposes, that does not make it land for all other purposes. Thus whilst the conveyancing *process* might be the same, it does not imply the actual underlying *asset* exists. As such the '15 year rule' is meaningless in so far as proving *title* to the Lordship.

Therefore so-called '15-year rule' is simply about aiding the conveyancing process. It does NOT prove the existence of the underlying title.

THIS PAGE IS INTENTIONALLY BLANK

5. *Registration of title with the Land Registry*

Before 13 October 2003, being the commencement of the Land Registration Act 2002, it was possible for Manors to be registered voluntarily with HM Land Registry. Despite this, most did not seek to register. Dealings in previously registered Manors are subject to compulsory registration, however lords of manors may opt to de-register their titles and they will continue to exist unregistered.

Registration of title with the Land Registry indicated who might be the registered proprietor of the title. However it is not conclusive proof. As shown in the Burton and Banford case, entry on the register is not conclusive proof, and indeed paragraph 5(a) of schedule 4 of the Land Registration Act 2002, enables the Registrar to alter the Register for the purpose of correcting a mistake therefore allowing for the fact that the Register may be incorrect.

As a result, registration of a Lordship of the Manor title with the Land Registry is not conclusive proof of ownership of that title.

After 13 October 2003, registration of a Lord of the Manor title was no longer possible.

THIS PAGE IS INTENTIONALLY BLANK

6. Trademark Registration with the Intellectual Property Office

This is the latest 'wheeze' thought up by some purveyors of Lord of the Manor titles as an attempt to 'prove' title ownership. They have used this to claim "government registration" of their "Lord of the Manor" titles.

Unfortunately, owning a trade mark does not give you ownership of the underlying asset. Trade marks are simply signs which can distinguish your goods and services from those of your competitors (you may refer to your trade mark as your "brand"). It can be for example words, logos or a combination of both. Trade marks are simply not registrable if they describe goods or services or any characteristics of them – so for example an attempt to trade mark "Lord of the Manor of X" would simply fail anyway when challenged.

As an example, a "Lord Sean Thomas Arthur Rafferty" tried to register as a trademark "Lord of the Manor of Fratton"[25], a Manor which was actually owned by someone else. The Intellectual Property Office confirmed that such a registration would

---

[25] http://www.ipo.gov.uk/t-find-number?detailsrequested=C&trademark=2645934

never be able to restrict the actual owner of the Manorial Title as the rights of that actual owner of the asset would trump the 'rights' of the alleged trademark holder – in other words, it doesn't confer ownership of the asset.

In any event, trade marks only have a life of 10 years and must then be renewed – whereas a real manorial title is a perpetual asset, a 'real' thing rather than a piece of intellectual property. In addition, Trade Marks cannot be inherited (which is why most are owned by companies), whereas a real Lord of the Manor title is an inheritable asset.

Therefore possession of a trade mark does not give you a Lord of the Manor title.

It has no more validity than changing your name to "Heinz 57" gives you ownership of the company which owns that particular brand or product range, and neither does it give you any claim whatsoever over its name or image rights.

Manorial Incidents

A Lord of the Manor may exercise certain rights usually known as 'manorial incidents'. Such rights could no longer be created after 1925. The main manorial rights can be summarised as:

- the Lord's sporting rights (for instance, giving the right to ride over land as a part of a Hunt, to shoot, or to manage fishing rights)
- the Lord's or tenant's rights to mining or quarrying
- the Lord's right to hold fairs and markets
- the Lord's or tenant's liability for the construction, maintenance and repair of dykes, ditches, canals and other works
- The Lord's ownership of unregistered land (known as 'manorial waste'.

These are just examples and it does not necessarily follow that such rights are legally exercisable.

Registered lordship titles at the Land Registry usually make no reference to any manorial incidents in the register. It may be that the benefit of the rights was not included in an earlier sale of the lordship title.

Under the Land Registration Act 2002 manorial rights are categorised as overriding interests, so a landowner is subject to them even if they are not mentioned in their register.

However, under s.117, these rights will lose their overriding status after 12 October 2013 (10 years after the Act came into force). Where any manorial rights have not been protected by notice or caution against first registration before 13 October 2013, they may not automatically cease to exist on that date and detailed guidance should be sought in these instances.

Claiming Manorial incidents needs to be proceeded with care, especially to ensure not only that they lawfully exist, but also that they have been correctly transmitted to the person intending to claim them

Of particular note is that until 1st January 1882, when the Conveyancing and Law of Property Act 1881 took effect, the conveyance of a reputed manor did NOT pass the freehold interest of the grantor in the waste of a manor, unless express words to that effect were used[26]. Part of the reason for that Act was to clean up the conveyancing process and to simplify the words required, so ensuring everyone was clear what was or was not included.

---

[26] Doe d Clayton v Williams (1843) 11 M&W 804, 807-808

These rights varied considerably, depending on the manor, the particular whims of the Lord when setting up tenancies, the predilections of their overlord and such like.

As such if you do intend to seek to claim these rights, make sure you carefully examine your purchase to ensure you don't waste a lot of time and money on a wild goose chase.

Therefore possession of a Lordship of the Manor title does not necessarily carry with it right to title of the manorial incidents or manorial waste. Equally possession of the rights to manorial incidents or rights does not necessarily carry with it rights to the Lordship of the Manor.

THIS PAGE IS INTENTIONALLY BLANK

1. Some interesting Manorial Rights

Having made those points – and noting that the chances are that any purchase you make neither has these rights, and even if they do you may well not be allowed to claim them – it is always an entertaining process to look at some of the more unusual manorial rights that did exist.

1.1 Foldage or Faldage

A right long gone, but especially popular in East Anglia, was the Lord's right to 'foldage'. Here, the Lord's tenants were required to pasture their sheep on his land.

This may seem a strange right to those unfamiliar with farming – but our agricultural readers will immediately spot the value of this.

Simply put, it meant that the sheep would be leaving their manure on the Lord's land – so fertilizing it and making it more productive. The tenants were not only deprived of this benefit, but then had to go and purchase their fertilizer from elsewhere – usually from the Lord. So the Lord gained a double benefit – and the tenants in effect had to pay twice for their fertilizer.

1.2 Estovers, botes, furze and turbary

Not so much interesting in content, but the names are lovely!

This refers of the right of the Lord to have various bits of natural fuel available on his manor. Estovers are wood and growing things used for building or fuel, botes are various rights to take wood from common land. Furze is a type of gorse and is useful for fuel and for fodder. Turbary is the right to cut turf of peat for fuel.

1.3 Pannage or mast

This refers to the right to acorns – a hugely valuable food for pigs in the medieval period. Given the size of the herds put out to pasture in the autumn this was a very valuable right.

1.4 Merchet

Often confused for *droit de seigneur* (the right of a Lord sleep with a village maiden on her wedding night – a right that never actually existed) is the right of merchet.

When the daughter of a serf was to marry someone from a different manor, her father needed the permission of the Lord. This is because if she stayed on the manor her children would also 'belong' to the Lord, whereas by leaving the manor her children belonged to a different Lord. As such her Lord needed compensating for the loss of their services.

Some manors also charged a fee (albeit smaller) for marriages between serfs within a manor.

Permission was always given – but there was always a fee. In 1350 in Pattingham in Staffordshire, merchet was set at 5 to ten shillings[27]. Given the average daily wage at the time was about 4 pence, this set merchet at between a week's and a month's wages.

1.5 Assizes of Bread and Ale

The Assize of Bread and Ale (Latin: Assisa panis et cervisiae) was a 13th-century statute which regulated the price, weight and quality of the bread and beer manufactured and sold in towns, villages and hamlets. Usually attributed to King Henry III, it was the first law in British history to regulate the production and sale of food.

---

[27] Hilton, R.H. (1975) The English peasantry in the Later Middle Ages (Oxford: Clarendon Press)Hilton, R.H. (1975) The English peasantry in the Later Middle Ages (Oxford: Clarendon Press)

This resulted in various local licensing systems, and indeed local standard 'pounds' and 'pints' determined by the Lord – along with arbitrary recurring fees, and fines and punishments for lawbreakers, and was enforced by the manorial courts.

This role is now carried out by Trading Standards Officers on behalf of local government. However a number of Lords of the Manor have a 'friendly' arrangement with local pub landlords to annually attend and 'test' the quality of the beers on offer, providing a good photo opportunity for the local media!

1.6 Stocks, Pillory and Cucking Stool

Lords of the Manor sometimes had the right to punish offenders by these methods, and in return had to maintain these in good working order[28].

---

[28] In 1684, the Lord of Calne himself was subject to a fine of £30 for having failed to maintain these in Calne borough. ('Calne: Local government', A History of the County of Wiltshire: Volume 17)

1.7 Gallows

Perhaps the one right many of us would like to claim is the "right of gallows" – or the right to execute capital punishment on offenders sentenced by the Lord as a result of a guilty verdict at the local court leet.

In the fourteenth and fifteenth century, some of George Washington's ancestors were feudal tenants of a Lord who held the right of gallows – and so the story of the creation of the United States of America may have had a very different story!

THIS PAGE IS INTENTIONALLY BLANK

Summary

In summary, ONLY ONE *traditional* method of proving ownership of a Lord of the Manor Title will actually give the right to the title:

> Holding a complete set of correctly written Deeds dating back to 3 September 1189 (or to the date of the formation of the Manor if the Manor was created between 1189 and 1290).

It is highly unlikely that any such document trail exists!

Not only must all the paperwork exist (and prior to 1925 it was not a legal requirement for Lords of the Manor to keep their paperwork), but IN ADDITION the right words must have been used in every single transfer of ownership.

Any slip up over the last one thousand years, and the entire chain simply ceases to exist – even if you have five or six hundred years of subsequent paperwork all apparently correctly written!

Some people have tried to rely on holding an incomplete set of documents – in some cases only going back up to 150 years. Providing no-one challenges the title, this may be acceptable to some. But is it really worth spending a significant sum of money on a pile of paper which still leaves you open to legal challenge?

Relying on this shortfall of paperwork leaves the 'owner' subject to challenge in the courts from anyone who claims a better claim to title – and as the Ireby Manor case proved there may be several different strands of potential owners who can challenge the Deeds.

Even if you do this, and win in court, this does not give you absolute ownership of the title. This is because the court does not have the power to confirm that you actually own the title. Its role is simply to confirm that you have the stronger right compared to the person against whom you are fighting.

So anything other than the dull set of properly written up deeds leaves you vulnerable. And as Ireby Manor proved, the court could even decide to strike off the manor as having been made extinct in history! So it is an inherently risky approach.

In reality, relying on either of these methods is likely to leave you with a significant headache and a large legal bill.

HOWEVER, all is not lost. There is still another method which is available to ensure you do have legal title to the TITLE of the Lord of the Manor, albeit without all the rights and land and so on – most of which have ceased to exist anyway. For all practical purposes it is only the Lordship Title that carries any real value now and into the future.

This method involved taking a step back and looking purely at the particular part of the Seigneury rights that most people today actually want – the title of 'Lord of the Manor'.

This is the method developed by the Liberty Hundred (http://www.liberty100.co.uk) for which they hold a Barrister's Opinion confirming its validity. Of course because it is commercially sensitive I can't talk about it openly in this book – but the Barrister employed to pick holes in the law says it works which is more than can be said for any of the other methods.

THIS PAGE IS INTENTIONALLY BLANK

About the Author

David Maximilian Cathmoir Nicoll is the 13th Baron of Bourn, and Lord of Adworthy. He is also a Freeman of the City of London, a Knight Grand Commander of the Order of St Edward, and is an honorary aide-de-camp to the Governor of the Commonwealth of Kentucky (a commissioned 'Kentucky Colonel', the highest honour awarded by the Commonwealth of Kentucky).

He is a former Midlands Business-Person of the Year and was also named the SFEDI Enterprise Champion Professional Service Provider 2009. He ran a high profile, award winning professional services and consultancy business until 2011 when he sold it on.

As someone with Aspergers Syndrome, David takes an obsessive interest in the intricacies of Manorial Law, and can't understand why there are so many people in the 'market' who get away with selling a pile of worthless paper. This book is his attempt to help the general public protect themselves against the smooth-talkers who are less than honest about what they are actually selling. ☺

Professionally, David is a Fellow of the Chartered Institute of Marketing and a Chartered Marketer, a Member of the Chartered Institute of Journalists, a Licensed Trainer of Neuro-Linguistic Programming^{TM}, and a Licensed Facilitator for Get Clients Now!^{TM}.

With a background ranging from small business start-ups to multinational companies, he specializes in helping businesses take the rule book and use it to their advantage – using the rules rather than being used by the rules.

Visit him on the web:

Web: www.david-nicoll.co.uk
LinkedIn: linkedin.com/in/dmcnicoll
Poken: https://user.poken.com/profile/1730955

February 2013